The Wild World of Animals

Whales

Giants of the Deep

by Adele D. Richardson

Consultant:
Jody Byrum
Science Writer
SeaWorld San Diego

Bridgestone Books
an imprint of Capstone Press
Mankato, Minnesota

Bridgestone Books are published by Capstone Press
151 Good Counsel Drive, P.O. Box 669, Mankato, Minnesota 56002
http://www.capstone-press.com

Library of Congress Cataloging-in-Publication Data
Richardson, Adele, 1966–
    Whales: giants of the deep / by Adele D. Richardson.
    p. cm.—(The wild world of animals)
    Includes bibliographical references (p. 24) and index.
    Summary: A brief introduction to whales, describing their physical characteristics,
habitat, young, food, predators, and relationship to people.
    ISBN 0-7368-1141-9
    1. Whales—Juvenile literature. [1. Whales.] I. Title. II. Series.
QL737.C4 R514 2002
599.5—dc21   2001003947

Editorial Credits
Megan Schoeneberger, editor; Karen Risch, product planning editor; Linda Clavel, designer
    and illustrator; Heidi Schoof, photo researcher

Photo Credits
Corel/Erik Stoops (texture), cover, 2, 3, 6, 8, 10, 12, 14, 16, 18, 22, 23, 24
Doug Perrine/Seapics.com, 6, 14, 18
Howard K. Suzuki/Seapics.com, 4
Ingrid Visser/Seapics.com, 10
James D. Watt/Seapics.com, cover, 1
Joe McDonald, 8
Phillip Colla/Seapics.com, 16
Robert Winslow/GeoIMAGERY, 20
Todd Pusser/Seapics.com, 12

1 2 3 4 5 6 07 06 05 04 03 02

Table of Contents

minke whale

eye

flukes

flipper

Whales

Whales are large sea animals. They have long, rocket-shaped bodies. Whales pump their flukes up and down to swim. They use the flippers on their sides to steer. Whales have an eye on each side of their head.

fluke

one part of the wide, flat area at the end of a whale's tail

sperm whale

Whales Are Mammals

Whales are mammals. Mammals are warm-blooded animals with a backbone. They have lungs. Whales breathe air into their lungs through blowholes on top of their head. This way of breathing makes them different from fish. Whales have either one or two blowholes.

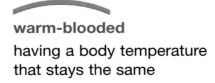

warm-blooded
having a body temperature that stays the same

blue whale

FUN FACTS

About 80 kinds
of whales live
in the world.

Whale Blows

Whales swim to the surface to breathe. Water sprays from their blowholes when they breathe out. This spray of water is called a blow. Whales sometimes can be identified by the shape of their blow. Blue whale blows are tall and thin. Gray whale blows are short and heart-shaped.

identify
to tell what something is

killer whale

Killer whales are part of the dolphin family. Dolphins are a type of whale. Killer whales are the largest dolphins.

A Whale's Habitat

A whale needs water for its habitat. Most whales live in oceans. Some whales swim in bays or rivers. Whales have a thick layer of blubber to keep them warm in cold water. Whales sometimes jump out of the water. This act is called breaching.

habitat

the place where an animal lives

gray whale

baleen

FUN FACTS

Baleen is made of keratin. Human fingernails also are made of keratin. People once used baleen to make umbrellas, fishing rods, and whips.

What Do Whales Eat?

Whales can have either teeth or baleen. Toothed whales use their teeth to catch fish or squid. Baleen whales have hundreds of thin plates in their mouths called baleen. They push mouthfuls of water through the plates. The plates trap tiny shrimplike animals called krill.

humpback whale and calf

FUN FACTS

Male humpback whales have songs that include squeaks, grunts, and other noises. Some songs are 30 minutes long.

Mating and Birth

Male and female whales mate every two to three years. A whale calf is born 9 to 17 months after mating. Female whales usually give birth to only one calf at a time. Some whales make noises to attract their mates. The noises sound like singing.

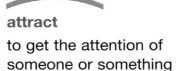

attract
to get the attention of someone or something

blue whale and calf

FUN FACTS

Blue whales are the largest animals that have ever lived. They are bigger than the largest dinosaur. The largest blue whale ever found was 110 feet (34 meters) long.

Whale Calves

Calves can see and swim as soon as they are born. They swim to the surface for their first breath of air. Calves drink milk from their mothers for 4 to 12 months. Calves stay near their mothers for at least one year.

pygmy killer whales

FUN FACTS

Whales do not chew their food. They swallow it whole.

Predators

Whales have few predators. Sharks hunt whales. Killer whales sometimes attack other whales. Toothed whales swim in close groups for safety. People once hunted whales. Some types of whales started to die out. Whale hunting now is illegal in many countries.

predator
an animal that hunts and eats other animals

beluga whale

Whales and People

Many people see whales in oceans and zoos. They watch whales play and perform. Some scientists study whales and their habitats. They then teach other people about whales. Scientists are working to make sure whales do not become extinct.

extinct
no longer living anywhere in the world

Hands On: Keeping Warm with Blubber

Whales have a thick layer of fat under their skin called blubber. Blubber helps keep whales warm in cold water. This experiment shows you how well blubber can keep whales warm.

What You Need

A bucket or sink
Cold water
A friend
Vegetable shortening

What You Do

1. Fill the bucket or sink with a few inches of cold water.
2. Hold out the first finger of one of your hands. Have your friend put a thick layer of shortening on it. Be careful not to get shortening on your other fingers.
3. Now dip the first finger of each hand into the cold water.

The finger with the shortening on it stays warmer than the finger without shortening. The blubber in a whale works the same way to keep the whale warm.

Words to Know

baleen (buh-LEEN)—thin plates in the mouth of some whales; baleen whales use their baleen to trap food.

blubber (BLUH-bur)—the layer of fat under the skin of a whale

flipper (FLIP-ur)—a paddlelike body part on a whale's side; flippers help whales steer through water.

fluke (FLOOK)—one part of the wide, flat area at the end of a whale's tail

krill (KRILL)—small animals that look like shrimp; baleen whales eat krill.

mate (MATE)—to join together to produce young; male and female whales mate to produce whale calves.

Read More

Cole, Melissa S. *Whales.* Wild Marine Animals! Woodbridge, Conn.: Blackbirch Press, 2001.

Greenberg, Daniel A. *Whales.* New York: Marshall Cavendish, 2000.

Kalman, Bobbie, and Heather Levigne. *What Is a Whale?* The Science of Living Things. New York: Crabtree Publishing, 2000.

Internet Sites

SeaWorld/Busch Gardens Animal Information Database
http://www.seaworld.org/infobook.html
Whale Tales
http://mbgnet.mobot.org/salt/whale/index.htm
Zoom Whales—All about Whales
http://www.enchantedlearning.com/subjects/whale

Index